MW01031155

Betta Fish Facts for Kids

Explore the Fascinating World of Betta Fishes and Learn Everything You Need to Know about Them

Table of Contents

Introduction 1

Chapter 1: An Introduction to Betta
Fish.. 3

Chapter 2: Meet the Betta Fish 11

Chapter 3: The Life of a Betta Fish 23

Chapter 4: Betta Fish Diet and Eating
Nutrition.. 29

Chapter 5: Betta Fishes Homes 36

Chapter 6: Betta Fish and Their
Personalities 43

Chapter 7: Fun and Educational Betta
Fish Facts... 50

Chapter 8: Betta Fish Care and Health 55

Conclusion 63

References 65

Introduction

Hey there!

Did you know that the betta fish is one of the most popular pets in the world? This unique aquatic creature is known for its energetic nature and colorful personality. You can't help but love it. Still, to keep them happy and healthy, owners must learn what betta fish like and dislike, how to care for them, and what to avoid doing around them. This awesome book is your guide.

Whether you have them as pets or simply want to learn what makes them great companions, this guidebook teaches you everything about the betta fish. By reading this book, you'll dive into the fascinating world of betta fish.

In simple words, the book explains where betta fish live in nature and how this place differs from their habitat in captivity. It teaches you how to feed them, keep them entertained, and spot when they feel unwell.

In a chapter dedicated to their personalities, you will get to know betta fish as pets and make friends. Bettas can be misunderstood because they're a little different from other fish. Fortunately, the book has a myth-busting section to help you understand who these small aquatic creatures truly are.

Even if this is your first time exploring the world of betta fish, this book explains everything in a way that makes it easy to understand. The instructions you are about to receive are easy to follow, especially with the helpful images. Continue reading if you are ready to begin this captivating journey awaiting you.

Chapter 1: An Introduction to Betta Fish

Take a deep breath and dive into the colorful world of the Siamese Fighting Fish. These wonderful creatures are known as labyrinth fish. The official scientific term for the vibrant little beings is Betta splendens, a combination of 2 languages: Malay for "Enduring Fish" and Latin for "Shining."

Some presume the name translates to "beautiful warrior," which is a fitting description of these tiny fighters.

1.   The betta fish is one of the most loved pets in the world. Source: https://upload.wikimedia.org/wikipedia/commons/thumb/9/95/Si amese-fighting-fish-bettas-1378308-hero-f459084da1414308accde7e21001906c.jpg/2048px-Siamese-fighting-fish-bettas-1378308-hero-f459084da1414308accde7e21001906c.jpg

The bettas are among the most common and loved pet options in the world. However, this hasn't always been the case. About 73 recognized species are within the genus Betta, with the Betta splendens being the most popular.

The bettas weren't always this beautiful and colorful. What you see and enjoy today results from years of selective breeding to produce the vibrant varieties of today's generation.

The Siamese fighting fish are known to be sensitive and complex little creatures that endure many hardships at the hands of pet traders. While many believe this fish is easy to own and care for, this couldn't be further from the truth. The Betta splendens require special care. Owning them can be quite costly.

Without the correct instructions on caring for them owners can mistreat the tiny warriors without meaning to.

However, with the correct information and love, you can learn to keep them happy, healthy, and content for years.

Betta Splendens Origins and History

Owning and breeding the Betta splendens have been a trend for a while. Some say the activity goes all the way back to the 14th century. During those ancient times, it wasn't unusual to see groups of people huddled over an aquarium, cheering, while a bloody battle ensued between 2 of these tiny fighters.

Bets were often made in these gatherings, and the sport became so popular that Thai royalty became interested. Today, fish fighting is banned in many countries.

Some people think that betta keeping started officially around 150 years ago in Siam (now Thailand), an exotic land in the heart of Southeast Asia.

It all started with some children looking for a game to pass the time. They decided to collect the little bettas in rice paddies, place them together, and watch as they bash each other in the small space. This little game is what earned the fish the title of Siamese fighting fish.

The fighting usually occurred between the male specimens - the females took no part in it.

The game grew over time and became so popular that the king imposed regulations and tax it.

Around 1840, the king of Siam gifted some fish to a Danish doctor, Dr. Theodore Cantor. The little creatures intrigued the physician, so he bred and studied them further.

2. *In 1840, the King of Siam gifted fish to Dr. Theodore Cantor.*
Source:
*https://upload.wikimedia.org/wikipedia/commons/4/4e/The_1st_*
King_of_Siam%2C_King_Mongkut%2C_in_state_robes%2C_Ban
gkok_Wellcome_V0037292_%28cropped%29.jpg

In the 1890s, the bettas made their way to France and Germany, and by 1910, they arrived in the United States of America with Mr. Frank Locke of San Francisco, CA.

A common misconception is that betta is pronounced similarly to the Greek letter Beta. The more logical belief is that their name is a tribute to the ancient Asian warrior tribe "Bettah," pronounced as "Bet-tah." If you're confused about how to say it, think of this sentence instead, "I feel better than yesterday."

Another name these fighters were called comes from Thailand, "Plakat," which means "biting fish." Again, a fitting name for the feisty little fellows.

Interesting Betta Features

You won't often see these mighty fighters in bowls together in the pet store. You wouldn't want to be the other fish in that bowl. The males are quite aggressive when placed with other fish in closed quarters. They chomp, injure, and sometimes kill the poor victim who was unlucky enough to live with them.

3. *The male betta fish are aggressive and this is why it's not good to have them together with other fish in the same bowl. Source: https://www.flickr.com/photos/scottkinmartin/484795442*

These feisty little fishes can do so much more than fight among themselves. They can breathe, for instance. Yes, you read that right. They can breathe oxygen just like you. While the newborns depend on their gills like other regular fish, the adults are a different story, thanks to their labyrinth organs.

That little body part is not so different from your lungs. It allows the bettas to swim to the surface for fresh air when bored of breathing underwater.

The bettas aren't only wonderful fighters and swimmers but also skilled jumpers. These guys can jump up as high as 3 inches out of water. However, not all their jumping is good. If the tank is poorly maintained and the conditions aren't to their liking, they sometimes jump out of it to escape.

Unlike most creatures in the seas or on Earth, bettas' maternal instincts lie with the fathers. The male species are responsible for building the bubble nest that lures the females. When the mothers are done laying the eggs, the males take care of the offspring and protect them, sometimes even from the mothers. They repair the nest and fetch the eggs that float away.

The Importance of Understanding and Appreciating Aquatic Creatures

Learning about interesting and unusual aquatic creatures like the Betta splendens is important for several reasons besides fun facts and unusual tidbits. Each being has a role to play in our environment, no matter how small they are. Your knowledge of the functions and mannerisms of these beings will help you protect them from abuse and help you understand the bigger picture of the mostly unexplored universe.

Yes, over 80% of the ocean hasn't been explored or mapped, and no one knows how many or what creatures, for that matter, dwell in its darkest depths. 80% of 70% of the Earth's surface is yet to be discovered. However, there are a few interesting facts that people do know.

4. So much of the sea has yet to be discovered and explored. Source: https://i1.pickpik.com/photos/797/799/755/fish-aquarium-sea-fish-tank-fb66ccfd93c10fd965944be97d3c0ca0.jpg

For instance, did you know that bodies of water store around 50% more carbon dioxide than the atmosphere? Did you also know that half the oxygen we breathe comes from the ocean?

Now, are you aware that aquatic creatures like dolphins, sea turtles, and sharks use carbon dioxide in the bodies of the ocean, allowing it to absorb even more from the air? This means they can help us fight against climate change, put a lid on the greenhouse effect, a cause of global warming, and reduce global problems like droughts and illnesses.

The balance of the marine ecosystem is vital to the balance of all life on Earth. You may think you're disconnected because those creatures live underwater, and you live on land. In truth, the impact of these creatures on humans and our actions toward them is enormous on both sides.

A well-known example of humans interfering with aquatic life and harming themselves is the coral reefs. Coral reefs are one of the water's most beautiful yet delicate ecosystems. Some people find it easier to fish around those reefs, causing significant damage and often death to those colorful beings. As they perish from the careless actions of humans, so do their services to protect us from erosion and dangerous weather fluctuations.

Not to mention that these reefs are homes and shelters for other aquatic animals, which then lose their habitat. If you're wondering how many there are, around 1 million species are estimated to depend on coral reefs for food and shelter.

You can learn so much from the underwater wonders. The tiny, mighty fighters, the bettas, can teach us about evolution, neurobiology, genetics, and the ability to adapt to harsh and unforgiving environments.

Chapter 2: Meet the Betta Fish

There are so many interesting facts about the tiny aquatic warriors. For one, the Betta splendens are among the most colorful fishes in the waters. However, they haven't always been like that. These tiny, vibrant, beautiful water dwellers didn't always sparkle and shine. In fact, wild bettas are known for their dull grayish-green, olive, and brown colors.

5.   *The wild betta is known by its dull brown and green coloring.*
Source:
https://upload.wikimedia.org/wikipedia/commons/d/d7/Betta_di
midiata_M005.jpg

Only through selective breeding was the world introduced to their rainbow-like resemblance.

So, how do you know you're looking at a freshwater anabantoid (ray-finned freshwater fish with a lung-like labyrinth organ)?

Varieties of Betta Fish and Their Vibrant Colors

There are so many varieties of the Betta splenden that it's almost ridiculous to keep track of them all. However, you can certainly try. Two main distinctions differentiate the bettas from each other: the color pattern and tail shape.

Colors and Patterns

The bettas come in many colors, like the rainbow of the sea. The most notable ones are:

1. Black Orchid Betta

Starting with the solid colors. The black orchid stands out from the rest for its elegance and subtlety. The body and fins are mostly covered in black, with streaks of blue running beautifully across its scales, adding a charming contrast to the jet-black background.

6.   The black orchid betta. Source:
https://www.flickr.com/photos/betta-online/1555650642

2. Mustard Gas

As the name implies, jets of yellow (mustard) and blue cover this little guy. This fish is a rare addition to the selective breeding performed around the 1990s. It took about 10 years of extensive experiments to get the look just right. The fins are usually covered in blue at the edges (sometimes brown), with the yellow springing out from the mid fin to the fish's body. It is replaced again by blue for the body's center and the head.

7.   The blue mustard betta is a rare and beautiful breed. Source:
https://www.pexels.com/photo/a-blue-mustard-betta-fish-in-an-aquarium-5150078/

3. Blue Betta

Blue is another solid color you would probably encounter more often than not in pet stores. There are different shades of blue, though: true blue, steel blue, and, of course, the brightest royal blue.

8. The blue betta. Source: https://upload.wikimedia.org/wikipedia/commons/8/81/Betta_sp lendens_%28blue%29.jpg

4. Cambodian Betta

These bettas are the belle of the party. They have a calm pinkish color covering their bodies, with angry red fins. In many cases, the pink is so pale it is as if you're looking at the flesh of the fish. Cambodian bettas were very popular among pet owners back in the day until breeders created them with brighter colors to replace this pattern.

9. The Cambodian betta. Source:
https://www.wallpaperflare.com/red-and-black-full-moon-betta-
fish-fighting-fish-three-color-wallpaper-zwdga

5. Butterfly Betta

This one looks like a butterfly. An exquisite-looking betta, well-known as a graceful swimmer. This fish is often categorized by one color that usually fades toward the fins. The fins turn white at the edges.

10. The butterfly betta. Source:
https://www.rawpixel.com/image/5913197/photo-image-public-
domain-blue-nature

6. Piebald Betta

It sounds mean to call these beautiful creatures bald. However, this type has a white or fleshy head with a solid color for the body that gradually gets darker from head to tail.

7. Koi Betta

It also goes by marble betta. This one gets its name from its resemblance to the Koi fish. So, if you're a Koi lover, consider getting this one. An interesting fact about this fish is that its colors change as it gets older. The little fish has 3 colors: white, orange, and black, with a spotted and blotched pattern. It can also be in red, yellow, and blue.

11. The Koi betta. Source: https://www.needpix.com/photo/download/998251/betta-fish-hmpk-free-pictures-free-photos-free-images-royalty-free-free-illustrations

8. Dragon Scale

One of the newer bred bettas, they are well known for the scales covering their bodies, resembling little swimming dragons. They have a shining metallic scale colored in silver on their bodies. The colors can vary from red to yellow to black between the tiny scales and all the way to the fins.

12. The dragon scale betta. Source:
https://www.flickr.com/photos/betta-online/1572014198

Other varieties of betta colors and patterns include the marble betta, the Bicolor, the Tricolor, the Dalmatian, and the solid colors of white, yellow, red, gold, and green, to name a few.

Tail Shapes

The bettas have intricately interesting tail shapes.

1. Elephant Ear Betta

Think of Dumbo when trying to picture this fish. Their one-of-a-kind appearance is cause enough to stare. Their pectoral fins look like a fan, often large, and stand out from the rest of the body. If the fish looks right at you, they look like elephant ears. However, aside from the beautifully shaped fins, they are not very agile swimmers. The size of their fins makes it better to live in still water so as not to have trouble fighting against a current.

13. *Elephant ear betta. Source:*
https://www.deviantart.com/bouzid27/art/betta-fish-8-729511014

2. The Crown Tail Betta

This exotic breed gets its name from the spiky-looking fins. The connecting webbing between the tail, dorsal, and anal fin is quite reduced. They look like spikes coming out of the fish.

Although they are easy on the eye, being a crown-tailed betta is not easy. They have a nasty habit of nipping their own tails. And in unfriendly and poor environments, the fin rays tend to curl. While better swimmers than the elephant variation, these guys also prefer still water to survive and be content.

14. The crown tail betta. Source:
https://www.flickr.com/photos/aquariumloto/7358868188

3. Plakat or Short Fin Betta

One of the smaller options, these bettas are known for their round bodies and short fins. They look more like the wild variety of bettas than the artificially bred ones. Some variations of the same kind have gone through selective breeding, like the half-moon and crown-tail Plakats.

15. Plakat or Short fin betta. Source:
https://upload.wikimedia.org/wikipedia/commons/thumb/7/72/D
VJ_Betta_splendens_006.jpg/2048px-
DVJ_Betta_splendens_006.jpg

4. Half Moon Betta

The large D or semi-circle-shaped tail is where this fish gets its name. The fins are rather large, and when fully flared, it looks like they're connected from the dorsal to the pelvic fins under the head. There are other variations of the same kind, like the over half moon, the delta tail, the super delta betta fish, and the half sun betta fish with its differentiating spiky tail.

16. Half moon betta. Source:
https://upload.wikimedia.org/wikipedia/commons/2/22/Betta_ha
lfmoon.jpg

Other types of bettas include the rose tail, the veil tail, the spade tail, the double tail, and the comb tail.

Physical Features That Distinguish Them from Other Fish

The naturally bred bettas, or wild bettas, look nothing like those in pet stores. In the late 1800s, scientists realized fighter fish display bright colors when provoked or agitated. They later found a way to keep the colors present and permanent.

Adult bettas are around 3 inches long, with a streamlined body that makes swimming look like a piece of cake, given that they are not paired with the more challenging fins like the elephant of dragon bettas.

The betta fish males, with longer fins, are commonly brighter than the females. Their colors flare more as they fight or mate. The males have a gill resembling a beard and are generally larger than the females. On the other hand, the females have shorter fins and, when ready to mate, display vertical stripes and an egg spot.

The scales on the betta's body are overlapping, transparent plates that protect the little fish from outside trauma and contribute to its graceful gliding. A thin mucus layer protects the scales from infections and parasites.

In the wild, the bright colors scare off predators and attract possible mates. When these causes are absent, the bettas return to their usual dull coloring of gray and brown. Selective breeding strips away the outside color of the betta to bring out the vibrant colors underneath.

The mouth of the betta is upturned to help them pick food from the water's surface. They use their fins to move and change directions smoothly in the water while maintaining a graceful balance.

Their fins consist of 1 caudal fin, 2 pectoral fins, 2 pelvic fins, 1 dorsal fin, and 1 anal fin.

Overview of Their Natural Habitats

The Siamese fighter fish initially come from Southeast Asia, specifically Thailand, in the Mekong basin of Laos. However, they can be traced to nearby countries, including Indonesia, Malaysia, Laos, Cambodia, and Vietnam.

The wild variety of bettas is found in shallow freshwater bodies like still ponds, rice paddies, calm streams, and marshes.

Accustomed to the warm weather of the east, the bettas thrive in temperatures around 80 Fahrenheit. Colder waters can cause them to stop feeding and become lethargic and vulnerable to infections and disease.

Chapter 3: The Life of a Betta Fish

Remember when you were a baby? Now you've grown up a little. Even your parents were once babies, too. They went from being in their moms' stomachs to coming out as tiny bundles of joy wrapped up in a blanket and grew until they became your parents.

From babies to children to teenagers, to young adults, and finally, adults - when you came into this world to meet them. This is what a life cycle is all about - the growth process from babies to adults. Fascinating right?

Like humans, animals also have a life cycle. They go from the baby stage to the adult stage. Now that you have met most of the betta fish species, it's time to learn about the life cycle of these colorful creatures.

Betta fish go through some pretty neat stages. In this chapter, you'll learn about the betta fish's stages of life and understand how these tiny warriors behave and interact. You'll be given tips on how to care for a betta fish in captivity. The door is open: come on in and learn about the betta warriors.

Life Cycle and Stages of Betta Fish Development

Watching your betta fish grow and spawn from the eggs is exciting. It usually takes a few weeks to a couple of months for the whole process to happen. If you've never seen it before or are merely interested, you're in the right place, It's time to explore how betta fish go from egg spawn to mature fish.

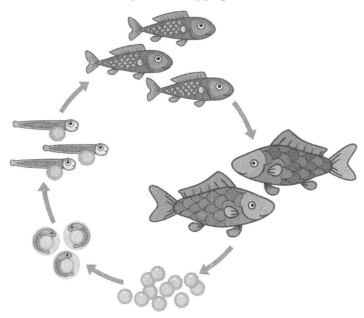

17. The betta life cycle. Source: https://www.istockphoto.com/vector/life-cycle-of-fish-sequence-of-stages-of-development-of-fish-from-egg-to-adult-gm1130099678-298778914

The Egg Stage: Betta fish start their life as tiny eggs. When a mommy and daddy betta fish love each other very much (or when a fish breeder puts them together), they do a little dance, and the mommy fish lays her eggs.

The daddy betta fish will first build bubble nests covered with mucus and then chase after the mommy. He shows off his bright colors and fins to attract her. Once he catches her, he'll wrap around her and fertilize eggs into her body.

These eggs are usually stuck to the underside of a bubble nest the daddy betta fish builds. It's like a cozy little nursery for the eggs to chill in until they hatch. Afterward, the female lays around 7 to 10 eggs, which the male collects and puts into his nest to protect like a good parent.

The Hatched Fry Stage: After a couple of days (usually around 2-3), the eggs hatch, and out come baby betta fish, called fry. These little guys are super tiny and can't swim very well at first, so they stick close to the bubble nest where it's safe. The daddy betta fish does a great job of protecting them and ensuring they're fed.

Nobody knows exactly how many fry will hatch – it could be anywhere from 1 to 300. The fry hang around their eggs and feed on them for about 24 hours before leaving the nest to live their lives. This is where the daddy betta fish has to say bye-bye and leave the tank.

The Mini Betta Stage: As the fry grows, they develop their fins and colors, but they are not very bright. But this is when you see their personalities shine through. During the first few weeks of their life, these babies, now known as juveniles, will explore their tank more and swim around like little pros. They also grow a labyrinth organ, which lets them breathe air.

They can reach up to an inch in length, but most will be closer to 0.6 to 1 inch. This stage lasts about 2 to 3 weeks before they grow very quickly.

The Young Adult Stage: This is the most important stage of their lives. They develop their bright colors, and their fins grow. Even though they're starting to look like adults, they're not ready to have babies yet. They're still not able to reproduce.

This stage lasts a few months before they become fully mature. During this stage, they are about seven to ten weeks old, and the growing process can last about three to four months.

The Full-Grown Stage: Your betta buddy is all grown up in this stage. Your betta fish is officially an adult when they can make more bettas. It means they're fully grown, usually around 2-3 inches long (like the size of your thumb).

You'll notice major changes in their behavior toward other fish. Especially the male ones – they get into chasing females, showing off their fins like they're flexing at the gym. It's like a fishy love story (or maybe a fishy fight club, depending on how you look at it). This full-grown adult stage is the longest part of their life, averaging 2-3 years. So, they're grown-ups for most of their time with you.

So, that's the life cycle of betta fish from egg spawn to mature adults. It's wonderful to watch them change and grow over time. And the best part is betta fish can live for a few years if they're well taken care of, so you'll have plenty of time to enjoy their company.

Understanding Betta Behavior and Interactions

Now, it's time to talk about how betta fish act and interact with each other. These fish are known for their feisty personalities – they're the tiny warriors of the fish world. In the wild, male betta fish can be aggressive toward each other, especially if they're defending their territory or trying to impress a ladyfish.

Therefore, it's necessary to keep male betta fish separate from each other unless you've got a big enough tank with plenty of hiding spots. Otherwise, they might get into some serious fights.

On the other hand, female betta fish are usually more relaxed and can live together peacefully in a group called a 'sorority' as long as they have enough space and hiding spots.

Betta fish are pretty smart and can recognize their owners. Some might even swim up to the glass to say hello when they see you approaching their tank.

They enjoy having places to hide and chill out. They like to sneak into plants or decorations in their tank when they want to take a break and relax.

Tips on Caring for Betta Fish in Captivity

Caring for betta fish is a big responsibility, but if you know what to do and how to take good care of them, they can thrive and live happy, healthy lives. Here are tips to keep your betta fish happy:

1. **Tank Setup:** Make sure your betta fish has a spacious tank with plenty of room to swim around. A tank size of at least 5 gallons is ideal for one betta fish.

2. **Water Quality:** Keep their water clean and toxins-free with regular water changes (about 25-50% of the tank volume every week). Ask your parents or a fish expert to help you here.

3. **Temperature and Filtration:** Betta fish are tropical fish and need their water to be warm (around 78-82°F). Get a good quality heater and filter to keep their environment stable and clean.

4. **Diet:** Give your betta fish a well-balanced diet of premium flakes or pellets, along with occasional treats like brine shrimp or frozen or live meals (bloodworms).

5. **Enrichment:** Keep your betta fish entertained by adding decorations, plants, and hiding spots to their tank. They love exploring and having places to hide and rest. Give them something to do, or they might get bored.

If you follow these tips and give your betta fish lots of love and care, you'll be rewarded with a happy and healthy fishy friend for many years.

Chapter 4: Betta Fish Diet and Eating Nutrition

Exploring the life of a betta fish will help you understand it better. Still, to care for your favorite pet, you must know its dietary and nutritional requirements. What does it eat? How much does it eat? How frequently should you feed it? This chapter dives into the betta fish diet and a few useful guidelines for feeding it. A few fun facts and secrets of these unique fish will also be revealed.

18. You need to find the best fish food for your betta's to live a healthy life. Source:
https://upload.wikimedia.org/wikipedia/commons/thumb/b/b3/3
-Colour_Fish_Food.jpg/2048px-3-Colour_Fish_Food.jpg

Exploring the Dietary Needs of Betta Fish

Betta fish have a large appetite, and they always seem to be hungry. They will keep gobbling up the food regardless of the quantity. However, overeating will cause several health problems, including indigestion, constipation, obesity, bladder issues, and even death. Did you know a betta fish's stomach is the size of their eye?

You should be very careful while feeding any fish, but it is even more crucial with betta fish. Since they are carnivores, they need a well-balanced, high-protein diet with other nutrients like fat, fiber, phosphorus, calcium, carbohydrates, and essential vitamins. Their food can be frozen live, freeze-dried, pelleted, or flaked.

- **Betta Pellets:** High-quality betta pellets are specifically formulated to meet the nutritional needs of betta fish. They contain a balanced blend of protein, fats, vitamins, and minerals. Look for pellets that list whole fish or fish meal as the primary ingredient. The tiny pellets expand in water, so don't overfeed your fish.

- **Freeze-Dried Bloodworms:** Freeze-dried bloodworms are a popular treat for bettas. These small, red mosquito larvae are rich in protein and are eagerly consumed by them. They should be fed as an occasional treat, not as a staple food.

- **Freeze-Dried Brine Shrimp:** Freeze-dried brine shrimp are another popular treat for betta fish. These tiny crustaceans are rich in protein and essential fatty acids. Like bloodworms, they should be offered as an occasional treat.

- **Frozen Foods:** Daphnia, brine shrimp, and bloodworms are great examples of frozen meals that provide diversity to your betta's diet. These foods are flash-frozen to preserve nutritional value and can be thawed (unfrozen) before feeding.

- **Live Foods:** Live food (bloodworms, daphnia, brine shrimp) can be fed for added stimulation and nutrition. However, live foods should be sourced from reputable suppliers to avoid introducing parasites or diseases into your aquarium.

- **Pelleted Flake Foods:** Some high-quality pelleted flake foods formulated for tropical fish can be suitable for bettas. Look for flakes that are specifically labeled for bettas or small tropical fish.

It is recommended to follow a standard feeding schedule for your betta fish.

Day	Food Type	Amount	Frequency
Monday	Pellets	2 to 4 pellets	1 to 2 times
Tuesday	Treats (live, frozen, or freeze-dried)	2 to 3 pieces	1 to 2 times
Wednesday	Pellets	2 to 4 pellets	1 to 2 times
Thursday	Pellets	2 to 4 pellets	1 to 2 times

Friday	Treats (live, frozen, or freeze-dried)	2 to 3 pieces	1 to 2 times
Saturday	Pellets	2 to 4 pellets	1 to 2 times
Sunday	Fasting Day	-	-

To aid with their digestion, it is important that betta fish fast one day every week.

Guidelines for Feeding Betta Fish to Promote Health and Vitality

You may follow the above feeding schedule religiously, but your betta fish may not. Use the trial-and-error method to find the ideal feeding schedule for your fish. Follow these guidelines to keep them healthy:

- Drop a couple of pellets in the tank early in the morning. If they finish it, give them a couple or three pellets in the evening.

- If your bettas aren't eating all the food, reduce the amount. For instance, if you gave the fish four pellets in the morning, of which it ate only two, either don't feed it in the evening or reduce the next day's amount to two pellets.

- Don't keep the uneaten food as is. It may attract bacteria that are harmful to your bettas. Either clean the water or scoop out the remains with a net.

- Betta pellets expand in the water, but it takes time. If the fish eat the pellets before that, they will expand in their tiny tummies, causing digestion problems. Soak the pellets in a separate water bowl, allow them to expand, and then introduce them to the tank.

- Don't follow the instructions on food packets and labels. They are applied to fish in general, not to betta fish. For example, "feed as much as your fish eats for 5 minutes" doesn't apply to betta fish. They may consume 5-10 pellets if you keep feeding them, but it may lead to bloating or obesity, and maybe even death.

- Invest in high-quality betta fish pellets as their staple diet. Look for pellets made explicitly for bettas, as they have essential nutrients tailored to their needs.

- While pellets should be the main component of their diet, they also enjoy variety. Offer goodies like brine shrimp, freeze-dried bloodworms, or live snacks like mosquito larvae every once in a while. This variety enriches their diet and mimics their natural feeding behavior.

- Pay attention to your betta's eating habits. Changes in appetite or behavior could indicate underlying health issues. If you notice abnormalities, adjust their diet and talk to a fish vet.

- Use a feeding ring to help your fish easily locate the food. It contains the food in one area of the tank, making cleaning easy if there are leftovers.

- Don't fret if you forgot to feed your betta fish. Did you know they can survive without food for a couple of weeks? So, they will be fine if you forget to feed them for a day or two. One or two days of fasting a week is also good for their digestion.

Fun Facts about Their Feeding Habits

- **Surface Feeders:** Betta fish prefer eating from the water's surface, not the tank's substrate. Their upturned mouths are adapted for this feeding behavior, allowing them to grab food from the surface easily.

- **Labyrinth Organ:** Betta fish are able to breathe air from the water's surface because they have a special labyrinth organ. They will often put it to use while feeding, as they gulp a gill full of air while eating the pellets from the surface. The labyrinth organ helps betta fish survive in oxygen-starved waters in their natural habitat, which includes rice paddies and small ponds.

- **Aggressive Eaters:** Betta fish are known for being aggressive, especially during feeding time. They may be territorial and flare their fins to dominate the area. Monitor their behavior during feeding to prevent aggression and ensure all fish receive their fair share of food.

- **Selective Eaters:** They can be quite selective with food. Some fish may prefer certain foods over others and even refuse to eat if the food doesn't appeal to them. So, introduce variety in their diet, especially with occasional treats (worms, larvae, insects, etc.)

- **Feeding Excitement:** Once your betta fish have become used to feeding at a certain time of day, they may show excitement when you approach the tank with the food. You may find them swimming eagerly to the surface in anticipation. It shows they understand the time and recognize you as their owner and friend.

Chapter 5: Betta Fishes Homes

Giving your betta fish a good home is as essential as a proper diet. You must understand their ideal habitat to build a good home. Native to Southeast Asia's shallow waters, betta fish are found in Cambodia, Laos, Thailand, and Vietnam. They mainly inhabit show-moving water environments like rice paddies, streams, ponds, and shallow pools, and they prefer to stay close to the surface. Don't wrinkle your nose there. You don't have to store your bettas in a muddy pool at home.

In this chapter, you will learn how to set up an ideal home for your betta fish, from the amount of water required to the environmental conditions needed. Your fish will live in great comfort after you're done building its home. A few handy maintenance tips for creating a healthy habitat are provided below.

Setting Up the Ideal Aquarium for Betta Fish

19. You need a few things to keep in mind when setting up the best aquarium for your betta fish. Source: https://www.needpix.com/photo/download/602745/betta-aquatic-freshwater-flamenco-free-pictures-free-photos-free-images-royalty-free-free-illustrations

You don't need to recreate the exact living conditions of your betta fish at home. For instance, they have learned to adapt to living in stagnant water, but they thrive in conditioned water rich in essential minerals. To create the ideal aquarium for your favorite fish, follow these tips:

- **Selecting the Tank:** Betta fish don't need a large tank but require a minimum of 2.5 gallons of water to survive. It's a bare necessity that will keep your fish alive, but they may not live happily. The recommended minimum is a tank that can hold at least five gallons.

- **Choosing Substrate:** You can choose gravel or sand substrate for your tank. Make sure it's smooth so it doesn't damage your betta's delicate fins. If you use something other than gravel or sand, ensure it is inert, meaning it shouldn't affect the minerals in the water. Try soft aqua soils.

- **Adding Water:** Fill the tank with dechlorinated water. Tap water can lower your betta fish's immunity, causing them to fall sick and even die. Use a water conditioner to remove chlorine and other harmful chemicals.

- **Setting Up Filtration and Heating:** Bettas are tropical fish and require a water temperature between 75-82°F. Install a small aquarium heater to maintain a stable temperature. A gentle filter is also recommended to keep the water clean but ensure its vibrations don't create waves and currents, as bettas prefer calm waters.

20. Aquarium heater. Source:
https://www.flickr.com/photos/homegardenlabs/14615464647

- **Cycling the Tank:** Before adding your betta, you must cycle the tank to establish beneficial bacteria to break down waste. You can do this by adding ammonia or using a bacterial supplement to kickstart the process. Cycling can take several weeks, so be patient.

- **Introducing Your Betta:** Once the tank is cycled and the temperature is stable, it's time to introduce your betta fish. Acclimate them to the new water temperature by floating their bag in the tank for 15-20 minutes. Then, release them gently into the tank and watch them spread their beautiful fins.

Decor and Accessories to Create a Comfortable Environment

A large fish tank isn't the only requirement to keep your betta fish happy. Imagine you are given a grand palace to live in, but there is nothing else there - no furniture, television, laptop, or water and electricity. You may roam around its big halls and explore every nook and cranny, but for how long? Eventually, you will get bored. This is precisely how a betta fish may feel without decorations and accessories. Add the following items to the tank to keep your fish comfortable and happy:

- **Plants:** Bettas enjoy having places to explore. Live or silk plants provide places for them to rest and feel secure. Avoid plastic plants with sharp edges that could damage their delicate fins.

- **Caves and Hideouts:** Adding caves, tunnels, or small structures to your tank gives your betta fish places to explore and hide. These decorations can help reduce stress and make them more cheerful.

21. *Betta fish need caves and hideouts in the aquarium to explore and hide. Source: https://www.flickr.com/photos/jelene/3007323784*

- **Driftwood:** Adding driftwood enhances the aesthetic appeal of your tank and provides hiding spots and surfaces for beneficial bacteria to colonize. Make sure the driftwood is aquarium-safe and properly cleaned and cured before adding it to your tank.

- **Floating Betta Logs:** Floating betta logs or hammocks provide resting spots near the water's surface. Bettas' labyrinth organ allows them to breathe air, so they enjoy resting near the water's surface.

- **Tank Dividers:** If you plan to keep multiple betta fish in the same tank, use tank dividers to separate them and prevent aggression. Ensure the dividers have small holes to allow water circulation and maintain water quality.

- **Lighting:** Bettas don't require intense lighting, but a gentle LED light can enhance your tank's visual appeal and promote live plants' growth.

- **Thermometer:** A thermometer is essential for monitoring the water temperature in your betta tank to ensure it doesn't fall below 75°F or exceed 82°F.

- **Water Conditioners and Test Kits:** Invest in a high-quality water conditioner to remove chlorine and other harmful chemicals from tap water. A water test kit helps you monitor water parameters such as pH (6.8 and 7.5), ammonia, nitrite, and nitrate levels.

Maintenance Tips for a Healthy Betta Fish Habitat

Like your house needs to be cleaned and maintained from time to time, betta fish tanks and accessories need the same care.

- Regularly change a portion of the water in the tank, around 20-30% of the tank volume every week. This helps remove accumulated waste and excess nutrients and replenishes essential minerals. Use a siphon to vacuum the substrate during water changes to remove debris.

- Using a reliable test kit, test water parameters like temperature, pH, ammonia, etc. Keep the water temperature between 75-82°F and maintain pH levels around 7.0. Ammonia and nitrite should always be at zero, while nitrate levels should be kept low through regular water changes.

- Remove uneaten food after a few minutes to prevent it from decomposing in the tank.

- Regularly clean the tank's glass or acrylic surfaces to remove algae buildup. Use an algae scraper or a soft sponge to clean the tank walls gently.

- Regularly check and clean the aquarium filter to ensure proper functionality. Replace filter media as needed according to the manufacturer's recommendations.

- If you have live plants in your betta tank, trim them to prevent overgrowth. Remove dead or decaying plant material to prevent it from fouling the water.

- Inspect all equipment weekly or monthly, including heaters, filters, and lights, to ensure they function properly. Replace malfunctioning or worn-out equipment to prevent disruptions in the tank environment.

- Monitor your betta fish for signs of illness or distress, such as lethargy, loss of appetite, abnormal swimming behavior, or changes in appearance. If you notice unusual symptoms, don't hesitate to contact a fish vet.

- Bettas have a tendency to jump, so make sure to keep your tank covered with a hood or top to keep your fish from getting out.

Chapter 6: Betta Fish and Their Personalities

Betta fish, like humans, have personalities that demonstrate their individuality. As their original name suggests, the Siamese fighting fish are naturally aggressive. If you put two betta fish in the same tank without a divider, they may fight for territory, and you will be left with only one. However, not all bettas are aggressive. Females are generally calm. Some species are naturally curious, whereas others can be as lazy as sloths. Observe your fish for a few days to determine its personality. It is much easier to see its individuality in its appearance.

Individuality among Betta Fish

Betta fish come in many colors and fin patterns. If you have purchased 10 betta fish, the chances are they all have a different appearance. Most varieties result from breeding and aren't found naturally in the wild. Some of the most common varieties include:

- **Veiltail Betta:** They are probably the most common betta fish. They have long, flowing fins that droop like a veil, giving them an elegant appearance.

22. The veil tail betta. Source:
https://www.flickr.com/photos/8113246@N02/4476169563

- **Crowntail Betta:** Another common breed, they have distinctive fins with reduced webbing, giving them a spiky appearance resembling a crown.

- **Halfmoon Betta:** They have large, fan-shaped tails that can spread 180 degrees when flared, resembling a half-moon shape.

- **Delta Betta:** They have tails similar to half-moons but don't spread out as fully. They have a more triangular or D-shaped tail when fully flared.

23. The delta betta. Source:
https://www.flickr.com/photos/aquariumloto/7358880052

- **Double Tail Betta:** They have a unique trait where their caudal fin (tail) is split into two lobes, giving them a double-tail appearance. They may have shorter bodies than other betta types.

- **Plakat Betta:** Known as "short-finned" bettas, they have shorter fins and tails than other betta types. They resemble the bettas in the wild more closely.

- **Rosetail Betta:** They have an exaggerated version of the crown tail trait, with their fins showing excessive web reduction, giving their fins a ruffled or rosette-like appearance.

24. Rosetail betta. Source: https://www.pickpik.com/red-fish-fish-underwater-aquarium-swim-abstract-91391

- **Elephant Ear Betta:** Their large pectoral fins look like an elephant's ears.

- **Dumbo Betta:** You may know the famous Disney character, "Dumbo" or "Jumbo Jr." with notably huge ears. The dumbo bettas are variants of elephant ear bettas, having some of the largest ears in the species.

- **Spade Tail Betta:** Spade tail bettas have tails like half-moons but with a slightly more pointed appearance, resembling the shape of a spade.

Unique Behaviors and Characteristics of Different Betta Personalities

While appearance defines much of their individuality, betta fish's behaviors and personalities make them who they are. In many other pets, like dogs, the animals reflect the owner's personality. But this is not the case with betta fish. Their unique personalities have nothing to do with the humans around them.

- **Aggressive:** This trait is often associated with male bettas, especially toward other male bettas or similarly colored fish. Some bettas may display heightened aggression, constantly flaring their fins and attempting to intimidate other fish in the tank. These need more care and should be given a separate compartment in the aquarium.

- **Territorial:** Bettas (mostly males again) can be highly territorial. They may fiercely defend their chosen territory, often marked by an object (like a large stone) or area within the aquarium. They might chase away intruders, including their reflection in the tank glass (which can be hilarious at times).

- **Curious:** Many betta fish are naturally curious and investigate their surroundings. They may interact with tank decorations, plants, or you outside the tank. Curious bettas may eagerly swim up to the tank glass when you approach, even during non-feeding hours.

- **Shy:** Some bettas are timider and prefer to hide among plants or other tank decor. They may come off as lazy since they spend more time in remote areas of the tank.

- **Playful:** A select few betta fish are playful. They may chase after floating objects or follow your finger along the tank glass. You would be very lucky to own one.

- **Calm:** This vividly contrasting trait is not too uncommon. Female bettas are generally calm and laid-back. They live peacefully with their tank mates.

- **Bold:** Certain bettas are bold and assertive, taking the lead in exploring their environment and interacting with other tank inhabitants. They may be more confident in their movements and less easily intimidated by changes in the tank.

- **Intelligent:** While fish intelligence is a topic of debate, bettas have demonstrated the ability to learn and recognize their owners and respond to training cues like feeding time. Some may seem particularly quick to learn and adapt to new situations.

Creating a Bond with Your Betta Fish

Betta fish may appear unsocial due to their aggressive nature, but they can build lasting bonds with their owners.

- **Regular Interaction:** Regularly spend time near the tank. Share your day with the fish like you do with your friend. Tell them what you did at school, what you had for lunch, and which subject you liked best. They may not understand you, but they get used to your presence and may recognize you as their caretaker over time.

- **Feeding Rituals:** Use feeding time to interact with your betta. They will quickly learn to associate you with food and may swim eagerly to the front of the tank when they see you approaching.

- **Consistent Routine:** Have a consistent routine for feeding and maintenance tasks. Bettas like predictability. So, a regular schedule can help them feel more comfortable and secure in their environment.

- **Avoid Stress:** Minimize stressors in your betta's environment, like sudden changes in water parameters or loud noises. A calm and stable environment will make them feel safe and secure.

- **Patience and Observation:** Building a bond with your betta takes time and patience. Observe their behavior closely to learn their preferences and habits and adjust your interactions accordingly. For instance, if they like the bloodworms more than other treats, include them in your feeding schedule twice a week.

Chapter 7: Fun and Educational Betta Fish Facts

You discovered interesting facts about betta fish in the previous chapters. They can breathe underwater thanks to their gills, and they can also breathe air thanks to a labyrinth organ that is located next to their gills. They prize their territory above everything else and don't mind fighting for it. More importantly, they are well-adapted to live in a muddy environment since they are found in puddles and shallow areas of slow-moving water.

25. Let's go through some amazing betta fish facts! Source: https://www.wallpaperflare.com/betta-fighting-fish-psychedelic-siamese-tropical-underwater-wallpaper-uayxj

This chapter will reveal the lesser known yet fun and educational betta fish facts that make these little dudes even more exciting. A few common myths will also be debunked. You will learn many entertaining games and activities centered on your betta fish.

Interesting Trivia about Betta Fish

- **The Name "Betta" Essentially Means Warrior**

    Forget Siamese fighting fish that spell out the creatures' nature. If you know a little about Southeast Asia's history, you will know that "Bettah" was the name of a menacing and powerful warrior clan in ancient days. It is probably how the fish (and their genus family) got their name in the late 1800s. Their scientific name, "betta splendens," translates to "beautiful warrior."

- **73 Different Species Have Been Discovered**

    Did you know that your favorite betta pet is one among 73 species? B. splendens may be the most popular bettas in the pet market, but many varieties are found in nature, from the smallest species of B. channoides (around one inch long) to the largest called B. akarensis (around five inches long).

- **They Can Jump Like Dolphins**

    Betta fish can leap out of the water. They can jump three inches above the surface and, on rare occasions, can get their entire bodies out of the water. They may not be as graceful as dolphins, but they look adorable while doing so.

However, it may mean the water quality has decreased or the tank is too small if they frequently jump. Clean the water or purchase a bigger tank right away. Also, cover the tank with a lid or hood so they cannot jump out.

- **They Can Be Trained to Perform Cool Tricks**

Again, betta fish may not perform as well as dolphins but are intelligent enough to learn a few cool tricks. You can train them to eat from your hand, swim through hoops, and rise to the surface for a pat on the head. You can organize a neat little performance with your betta the next time your friends come for a sleepover.

Myth-Busting Common Misconceptions

Betta fish have shown a great rise in popularity as pets in recent years. This popularity has led to several myths about the creatures. Many are downright harmful.

- **Betta Fish Can Thrive in Small, Unfiltered Bowls**

This is one of the most common myths. While bettas are hardy, adaptable fish, they require sufficient space, filtration, and water quality to thrive. All this isn't found in small bowls or vases. They can survive in confined spaces, but they won't thrive there. They won't be happy.

- **Betta Fish Prefer to Live Alone**

While male bettas are territorial and aggressive toward other males, they can coexist with other fish species. Female bettas can live peacefully in groups.

However, you must research tank mates carefully to ensure compatibility and prevent aggression.

- **Betta Fish Don't Need Water Changes**

    Some people believe that betta fish don't require regular water changes because they can breathe from the surface. However, like all aquarium fish, bettas produce waste that gathers in the water, leading to ammonia buildup and poor water quality. To keep the ecosystem in the tank healthy, add important minerals, and get rid of pollutants, regular water changes are required.

- **Betta Fish Prefer Dirty Water**

    While bettas can tolerate lower water quality than other fish species, they still require clean water. Contrary to popular belief, bettas are not found in "dirty" water in the wild but in "muddy" water rich in essential minerals. There is a significant difference. Hence, regular water changes and proper filtration are necessary to keep them healthy and happy.

Educational Games and Activities for Young Readers

You don't need to read huge manuscripts to learn about and play with your new favorite pet. Organize simple activities and games in your pet group, or try to train your betta fish. Here are a few ideas:

- **Follow the Finger**

    Do you regularly interact with your betta and feed it every day? It would have recognized you as its caretaker by now. Run your index finger along the side of the tank back and forth. If it follows your finger, it accepts you as its caretaker.

- **Swimming through a Hoop**

    Hold a plastic hoop with a string just below your tank's water surface. If your betta is on the left side of the tank, drop a food pellet on the right so that the hoop is between the betta and the pellet. As it swims toward the food, adjust the hoop in its path so it swims through it.

    With enough practice, it will learn to swim through the hoop wherever it's placed when you feed it. When this becomes routine, hang the hoop just above the surface to make your betta jump out of the water and through the hoop.

- **Betta Fish Matching Game**

    Ask an adult to create a matching chart for you or your friends. You need to match betta fish-related terms with their definitions or images. For example, you can match terms like "labyrinth organ" with its function of "allowing bettas to breathe air from the surface" or with its picture. This game can help improve your vocabulary and understand concepts related to betta fish care and biology.

- **Trivia Game**

    In your pet group, create a trivia game with questions about betta fish anatomy, behavior, habitat, and care requirements. Players take turns answering questions, and you can award points for correct answers. It is an interesting way to spread awareness and knowledge about your new pet.

Chapter 8: Betta Fish Care and Health

To properly care for a betta, you must learn to spot signs when they feel unwell. This chapter discusses common health issues of betta fish, their signs, and what to do when you notice them. It provides tips for keeping your betta happy and free from stress and to be a responsible owner.

26. You want to make sure you're taking the correct steps to take care of your betta fish. Source: https://unsplash.com/photos/male-and-female-blue-and-red-fighting-fish-oX_kRW8Cjok

Common Health Issues and How to Address Them

Understanding their health issues is crucial for caring for a betta fish. Spotting the signs early and knowing how to treat them will help prevent bigger issues and give your betta a long and healthy life.

You'll likely interact with your pet every day, so when you do, look out for these warning signs that your betta is unwell:

- Bloated or hollow belly
- Loss of appetite
- Bulging eyes
- Torn or split fins or tails
- The fish sinking, floating or swimming strangely or uncoordinated
- Changes in color (in a specific body part or the entire fish)
- Slow movement and lack of interest in playing
- Rapid breathing or gasping
- Clamped fins
- Horizontal stripes
- Scratching against surfaces in the tank

Below are a few common health issues these signs indicate:

Ich

This is a serious illness caused by a parasite. You can spot ich by small white spots on your betta's body and fins. You might notice that your fish rubs their body against the glass, substrate, or decoration more often than usual. They might also eat less or hide.

Your betta needs medication to expel the parasite from their body. Ensuring they're nice and warm, changing their water frequently, and adding plenty of aquarium salts to their water are excellent ways to address this condition.

Flukes

Flukes are caused by parasites that feed on the betta's skin and gills, making them itch. The main symptom is the fish scratching against the rocks and other sharp objects in their habitat.

This serious condition must be treated with specific medication, but adding aquarium salts to their water can help them heal faster and relieve their itching.

Velvet

Known as Gold Dust Disease, Velvet is another condition caused by parasites. This common and serious disease makes your betta look like their body is covered in gold. Your fish might be missing some scales and have red skin in these places. Velvet can damage the betta's gills, making them breathe faster.

Copper sulfate medication will treat Velvet. Reducing the light and increasing the heat also helps.

Anchor Worms

Parasites like anchor worms attach to the fish's skin, injuring and making it bleed. The worms can be removed with tweezers, and aquarium salts can help the fish heal faster.

Fungal Infections

Fungal infections are common in bettas. While they don't cause much problem in healthy fish, fungi can lead to serious health issues in injured animals. You can spot fungal infections on your pet by a soft white or gray fuzzy growth on their body, fins, or gills.

Too many fungi in the aquarium cause fungal infections, so the first step in treating them is to remove the fungi by frequently filtering the water. Your fish will likely need antifungal medication, too.

Fin Rot and Tail Rot

If your fish is injured, they can get a fin or tail rot. Bettas have long, delicate fins easily damaged by getting too close to sharp plastic decorations. The fish will have visible injuries like splits or rips on their tail and fins. Their injury can get infected, causing tail and fin rot. If fungi cause the infection, the fish will have a cotton-like growth on the injured part. If it's bacteria, the injured part will have a different color.

The condition is caused by poor water quality, so increasing filtration and adding aquarium salt are great ways to help the fish. Then, depending on whether fungi or bacteria caused the infection, the fish is treated with antifungal medication or antibiotics.

Swim Bladder Disorder

Some bettas can be affected by Swim Bladder Disorder, making it difficult for them to swim. Your fish will float on their side, swim upside down, or sink to the bottom of the aquarium.

The condition is caused by poor water quality, diet, and low temperatures. Improving water quality by frequent filtration and paying attention to proper feeding can help treat them. Also, remove anything causing them stress.

Bloating

If your betta has a bloated belly on one or both sides of the body, this might have different causes. It may simply be that you aren't feeding it right, so it gets constipated, or it can have an infection causing it to bloat. Egg holding can also lead to bloating.

The best way to treat bloating is to observe your fish to see if other signs will reveal the condition. For example, bloating caused by poor feeding can be treated with Epsom salt.

Popeye

Infection or injuries can cause the betta's eyes to bulge. This condition is known as Popeye. As scary as it looks, it often goes away on its own, especially if it's caused by a small injury, which is likely if it's only on one side. Monitoring your fish's condition is necessary.

If it's on both sides, it might be caused by bacterial infection, which needs to be treated with antibiotics and proper water filtration.

Tips on Keeping Betta Fish Happy and Stress-Free

27. Just like any other pet, you have to take the time to give your betta fish attention. Source: https://www.pexels.com/photo/small-girl-enjoying-goldfish-in-the-aquarium-8434686/

The best way to prevent illnesses and injuries is to keep your betta happy and stress-free. Here are a few tips:

- Make sure your tank is big enough for the bettas to swim around, as these fishes need a lot of exercise and will be in a small space.

- If you're getting a new fish, cycle your water beforehand.

- Change the water frequently as bettas are sensitive to poor water quality — and check the water regularly.

- Clean the waste, unwanted food, and other debris with an aquarium vacuum, as bettas don't like a dirty space.

- Make them comfy with plenty of plants and decorations for hiding and playing around.

- Offer them a varied diet. They don't like to eat the same food all the time.

- Talk to them — they will be happy to hear your voice, especially when you feed them.

- Add interactive toys like floating mirrors to keep your betta active.

- Keep a consistent routine by feeding them at the same time daily and cleaning their tank on the same day of the week.

- Give them caves and other places where they can hide and feel safe.

- Keep them warm with a water temperature of between 75°-82°F.

- Change their environment occasionally to keep things interesting.

Responsible Ownership and Ethical Considerations

A responsible owner should know what not to do around bettas. Here are a few mistakes to avoid to ensure your pet is healthy and happy:

- Don't forget to change their water regularly because harmful fungi and bacteria accumulate quickly.

- Don't use coverless aquariums because bettas are sensitive to changes in water quality. You can't control what gets into the water with an open tank.

- Use the right size filters. Otherwise, your fish can get injured by a powerful current or by being pushed around during filtration.

- Don't use sharp plants and decorations, as these can injure your pet.

- Don't forget to cycle the tank if you move your pets to a new home.

- Don't force your betta to share their home with a tank mate with bright colors or long fins or is aggressive because they will fight all the time, leading to injuries.

Conclusion

By reading this book, you've learned about the betta fish - where it comes from, what makes it different from other fish and aquatic animals, and their different features.

You explored their natural habitat and peeked into their lives, seeing how they develop into the unique animals they are, how they interact with each other and other fish, and how to make them happy in captivity.

You've learned how to feed betta fish properly and avoid feeding mistakes that could make them unhappy and unhealthy. Remember, betta fish have unique feeding habits, and caring for their nutrition is quite a journey.

The same goes for ensuring they like their homes. They don't want to be bored, so owners need to switch things occasionally to keep them entertained. It's a wonderful opportunity to make friends with the fish and learn more about what they like. They might be small creatures, but they certainly have big personalities.

You read interesting facts about betta fish, their traits, and the myths surrounding them. Knowing what they like will help you on the right path if you plan to make friends with your betta fish.

Lastly, you learned about common health problems in betta fish. Knowing how to spot the signs they are unwell is half the battle to fight off what ails them.

Whether you care for your betta fish or simply want to learn more about these aquatic creatures, now you know everything about them. Thank you again, and please share what you think of this book.

References

Adams, C. (2017, August 15). How To Set Up A Betta Fish Tank (Step-by-Step). Modest Fish. https://modestfish.com/how-to-setup-first-betta-fish-tank

Admin. (2023, May 22). Betta Fish: Understanding Their Feeding Habits. Onyx Aqua Farm. https://onyxaqua.com/betta-fish-understanding-their-feeding-habits

Aqueon. (2021). The Fascinating Origin of Betta Fish and Other Fun Betta Facts. Www.aqueon.com. https://www.aqueon.com/articles/origin-of-betta-fish-and-facts

Benard, A. (2024, January 11). How to Take Care of a Betta Fish (with Pictures) - wikiHow Pet. Www.wikihow.pet. https://www.wikihow.pet/Take-Care-of-a-Betta-Fish

Betta Fish Care. (2021). Adelphi.edu. https://home.adelphi.edu/~ve21375/Betta%20Fish%20Care.html

Betta Fish Tank Setup. (2022). Aqueon. https://www.aqueon.com/articles/betta-fish-tank-setup

Betta Fish, Facts and Information. (2022, May 4). Animals. https://www.nationalgeographic.com/animals/fish/facts/betta-fish

Betta Fish: Facts and Why They're Not "Starter Pets." (2019, September 19). PETA. https://www.peta.org/features/never-buy-betta-fish-as-pets-how-siamese-fighting-fish-suffer/

BettaInfo. (2017, February 17). Betta Fish Tail Types - Japanesefightingfish.org. Japanesefightingfish.org; Japanesefightingfish.org. https://japanesefightingfish.org/betta-fish-tail-types/

Blake, M. (2023, August 2). Do Betta Fish Recognize and Interact With Their Owners? | LoveToKnow Pets. LoveToKnow. https://www.lovetoknowpets.com/aquariums/do-betta-fish-recognize-interact-their-owners

Bryan. (2016). Betta Fish | Advocating For Proper Care & Information. Bettafish.org. https://bettafish.org

Bryan. (2017, November 26). Betta Fish Care - How to Take Care of a Betta | Bettafish.org. Bettafish.org. https://bettafish.org/care/

Bryan. (2024, February 23). Best Betta Fish Food | What to Feed & How Much. Bettafish.org. https://bettafish.org/care/food-feeding

Buddy, B. (2023, May 19). The Miraculous World of Betta Fish Eggs: A Deep Dive into Life's Tiniest Wonder. Medium. https://medium.com/@BettaBuddy/the-miraculous-world-of-betta-fish-eggs-a-deep-dive-into-lifes-tiniest-wonder-3da1a5fe9629

Byrkley Aquatics. (2023, March 10). Keeping Your Betta Fish Active and Happy: Tips for Enrichment and Exercise. Byrkley Aquatics. https://www.byrkleyaquatics.co.uk/post/keeping-your-betta-fish-active-and-happy-tips-for-enrichment-and-exercise

Campbell, C. (2023, March 31). Top 5 Mistakes to Avoid as a Betta Fish Owner. PetHelpful. https://pethelpful.com/fish-aquariums/Mistakes-I-Made-as-a-Betta-Fish-Owner

Dockett, E. (2023, April 4). What Do Betta Fish Eat? A Betta Feeding Guide for Beginners. Pet Helpful. https://pethelpful.com/fish-aquariums/What-Do-Betta-Fish-Eat-Feeding-Guide

Fabian. (2020, January 13). Betta Fish Growth Stages - From Fry to Adult. SmartAquariumGuide. https://smartaquariumguide.com/betta-fish-growth-stages/

Fishies, S. (2020, October 13). Finding Your Betta's Personality for the Best Tank Mates. Medium. https://medium.com/@spycat/finding-your-bettas-personality-for-the-best-tank-mates-27abb86f6121

Fores, J. S. (2022, December 21). 15 Common Betta Fish Diseases (With Photos): Prevention and Treatment. PetHelpful - by Fellow Animal Lovers and Experts. https://pethelpful.com/fish-aquariums/diseases-of-a-Betta-fish

Gibbins, F. (2023, August 4). Betta Fish Jumping: 4 Reasons Why Your Pet Is Hyperactive. Https://Japanesefightingfish.org/. https://japanesefightingfish.org/betta-fish-jumping

Hosmer, A. (2022, July 11). 10 Myths You Might Believe About Betta Fish. Dustin's Fishtanks. https://dustinsfishtanks.com/blogs/dustins-blog/betta-fish-myths

The Spruce Pets (2019). Learn Everything You Need to Know About Betta Fish. The Spruce Pets. https://www.thesprucepets.com/siamese-fighting-fish-bettas-1378308

Morgan, K. (2020, January 4). Betta Fish Facts You'll Love To Share. Modestfish.com. https://modestfish.com/betta-fish-facts

Nippyfish. (2017, September 27). Betta Growth from Birth. Fish Care. https://nippyfish.net/2017/09/27/betta-growth-from-birth/

Page |, A. (2021, July 9). 17 Tips to Have a Happy Betta Fish. Tankarium. https://www.tankarium.com/happy-betta-fish/

Petch, D. (2022, June 30). 10 Fun Betta Fish Facts. TrustedHousesitters. https://www.trustedhousesitters.com/blog/pets/betta-fish-facts/?gad_source=1&gclid=CjwKCAiAlJKuBhAdEiwAnZb7lS-PxYo9i3Wp7ozsHL_jDEuDyGUfDcRHT_bjgaoRXvyZZUodoG3fixoCksQQAvD_BwE

Priyadarshika. (2022, April 12). Facts & Information about Sea Animals for Kids. Firstcry Intelli Education. https://www.firstcry.com/intelli/articles/sea-animals-for-kids-teach-your-child-about-ocean-animals/

Reptile Pedia. (2023). What Is a Good Betta Behavior? Www.reptileknowledge.com. https://www.reptileknowledge.com/reptile-pedia/what-is-a-good-betta-behavior

Roth, A. (2021, May 14). The 1,000-Year Secret That Made Betta Fish Beautiful. The New York Times. https://www.nytimes.com/2021/05/14/science/betta-fish-breeds.html

scalestails. (2013). Betta Myths Debunked. Tumblr. https://scalestails.tumblr.com/post/53150684212/betta-myths-debunked

Shimmer. (2022, May 7). What Is the Normal Betta Behaviors - Hygger. Hygger. https://www.hygger-online.com/what-is-normal-betta-behavior/

Stanton, L. (2018, June 6). The History of Betta Fish (Origins & Landmark Moments). Hepper. https://www.hepper.com/the-history-of-betta-fish/

Stanton, L. (2019, November 9). 37 Types of Betta Fish: Breeds, Patterns, Colors & Tails (With Pictures). Hepper. https://www.hepper.com/types-of-betta-fish/

Sterling, I. (2019, February 3). Best Betta Fish Tank Size -The Wrong Size Can Kill Your Fish. Fish Lab. https://fishlab.com/betta-fish-tank-size

Sturgeon, D. (2019). Betta Splendens (Siamese Fighting Fish). Animal Diversity Web. https://animaldiversity.org/accounts/Betta_splendens/

The Aqua Advisor Editorial Team. (2021, March 24). Betta Fish Personality: Everything You Need to Know. The Aqua Advisor. https://theaquaadvisor.com/betta-fish-personality

The Fascinating Origin of Betta Fish and Other Fun Betta Facts. (n.d.). Www.aqueon.com. https://www.aqueon.com/articles/origin-of-betta-fish-and-facts

Valderrama, M. (2021, December 14). 15 Types of Betta Fish (with Pictures!) - AquariumStoreDepot. Aquariumstoredepot.com. https://aquariumstoredepot.com/blogs/news/types-of-betta-fish

Valderrama, M. (2023, June 9). Most Common Betta Fish Diseases - 11 Most (And How To Cure Them). Aquariumstoredepot.com. https://aquariumstoredepot.com/blogs/news/betta-fish-disease

What If There Were No Coral Reefs? (2023, November 22). SEA LIFE London Aquarium. https://www.visitsealife.com/london/information/news/what-would-happen-if-there-were-no-coral-reefs/#:~:text=If%20all%20coral%20reefs%20were

What Is Marine Life And Its Importance? Facts & Statistics - GenV. (2021, November 30). Https://Genv.org/. https://genv.org/marine-life/

Made in the USA
Monee, IL
20 November 2024

70738394R00046